ASIAN COOKING MADE EASY
Indonesian

JENNY FANSHAW & KERRY KENIHAN

APPLE

An R & R Publications Marketing
Pty Ltd book

First published in the UK by
Apple Press in 2006
Apple Press
Sheridan House
114 Western Road
Hove
East Sussex BN3 1DD

www.apple-press.com

Asian Made Easy: Indonesian
was created and produced by R & R
Publications Marketing Pty Ltd
12 Edward Street, Brunswick, Victoria
3056, Australia
Email: info@randrpublications.com.au

Publisher: Richard Carroll
Production Manager: Anthony Carroll
Food Photography: Craig Cranko
Travel Text: Kerry Kenihan
Photography of Indonesia: Stock Photos
Pty Ltd
Food Stylist: Liz Nolan
Assisting Home Economist: Jenny
Fanshaw
Recipe Development: Jenny Fanshaw
Cover Design: Jane Waterhouse
Text Designer: Lucy Adams
Computer Graphics: Elain Wei Voon Loh
Editor: Fiona Brodribb
Proofreader: LoftCom

ISBN-10: 1 84543 127 8
ISBN-13: 978 1 84543 127 3

Printed in Singapore

10 9 8 7 6 5 4 3 2 1

CONTENTS

the land AND ITS PEOPLE

Status	Republic
Area	1 919 445 sq km
Population	179 300 000
Language	Bahasa Indonesia
Religion	Muslim
Currency	Rupiah
National Day	17 August

PREPARE FOR EXCITEMENT

On the beaches of Indonesia, before the sun has risen, bare-chested, barefooted fishermen still wear the coolie-style hats that protected them from the previous day's piercing sun. After an intense night's labour at sea, they closely examine their catches.

Indonesia is one of the world's poorest countries but has one of the richest cuisines and an abundance of natural resources. These resources include spices, rice (the staple), coffee, sugar, tobacco, teak, sandalwood, copper and bronze.

There are many such gatherings of fisher-folk who could be members of the Muslim, Buddhist, Hindu, Christian or animist faiths. The fishermen of Indonesia represent an unprecedented 336 ethnic groups in a nation freed from colonialism since 1947 and dictatorship since 1999. Their skin colours vary from jet black to pale brown. An astounding 500 languages and dialects are spoken but bahasa Indonesia, the national language, is taught in Indonesian schools. About 70 per cent of Indonesian people are fluent in this language.

Indonesia's fishermen, including those based on fragile wooden rigs on atolls or anchored at sea for weeks or months on end, have 200 million people to feed. Indonesia land mass is about eight times bigger than the United Kingdom and the fishing grounds in surrounding seas are estimated to be four times larger again.

Indonesia is the world's largest archipelago. It extends for about 5 600 km from the Indian Ocean into the Pacific. There are more than 13 600 separate islands. Most are emerald-green with tropical rainforests or rice paddies amid volcanic eruptions; a few are bare deserts.

Indonesia has been influenced by the cultures of China, India, Arabia, Portugal, Spain, England, America and the Netherlands. People from these countries mostly arrived in the form of explorer–traders in quest of spices. During World War II, the Japanese also occupied Indonesia for a time; several Japanese culinary influences still linger.

The Dutch dominated Indonesia for 350 years from the 17th century, so a fascinating amalgam of cuisines emerged. The Dutch, bland cuisine was much the richer after integrating with Indonesian cuisine. Rijstafel (Dutch for rice table) is an enormous buffet of rice and blends of dishes originating from Holland and Indonesia. Rijstafel was probably the western world's first introduction to Indonesian cuisine before Bali became known as the most bountiful, most

beautiful, budget beach tourist destination any hedonist could want. So Indonesian cuisine burst into the most adventurous kitchens on the planet. It was chilli-hot, spicy with cool contrasts, festive, fun to prepare and fabulous to eat.

Sumatra, Java, Bali, Irian Jaya, Kalimantan, Sulawesi and Maluku along with their islands and those of Nusa Tenggara, have diverse ethnic and culinary traditions. In this book we have gathered together dishes from all over Indonesia to give you a taste of the wonderful and varied cuisine of Indonesia.

DAY BY DAY

Each Indonesian family endeavours to eat at least three plates of rice each day; note *plates*, not bowls. If plates are not available nor affordable, disposable banana leaves are used. The implements are fingers (of the clean right hand). Chopsticks are never used with traditional cuisine, though

Indonesians may eat with a spoon and fork.

There is little difference between breakfast, lunch and dinner in Indonesia. It is all a question of availability and affordability, so the food may be the same but in varying quantities; always served with rice. Meat, fish and vegetables will be served in fast succession, not together in Chinese-style. However Indonesians can produce the most tempting and fantastic buffet dinners after sunset. Like Chinese meals, the ingredients in an Indonesian buffet are composed of contrasting dishes; hot and spicy versus mild; sweet versus sour; fried food balanced by a superlative steamed dishes.

As is the custom in many Asian countries, it is polite in Java and Bali for guests to leave left-over grains of rice to indicate their gratitude and satiation to the hosts. The hostess, often the cook, may well appreciate left-over rice as it could be used the next day in what is regarded as Indonesia's national dish, *nasi goreng* (fried rice).

The land and
ITS PEOPLE

With its religious diversity, Indonesia's festivals are many. Prominent feasts are held mid-year to celebrate harvest, not with rice but, (especially in Bali and Sulawesi) with pig and /or buffalo meat barbecued on bamboo tubes. (Muslims do not eat pork.) The meat is accompanied by copious amounts of white or red *tuak*, a cloudy sweet-sour palm juice wine.

Non-Muslims like an evening tipple or three of home-brewed *tuak*, which men imbibe while smoking clove-scented cigarettes. In Bali, beware; their glutinous rice wine (pink and drunk with coconut juice) and rice brandy are potent and potentially dangerous. It's best to stick with local or imported beer or warm or cold tea. The Dutch introduced good coffee-making techniques in the late 1600s and Indonesians have added their own stamp with ground peanuts. If this sounds good, try it out!

Daily food in
INDONESIA

SILAKAN MAKAN, SILAKAN MINUM

These words are encouragements to 'Please eat, please drink,' to be uttered when your guests sit at the table to partake of your own, home-cooked Indonesian feast. It may be a *rijstafel*, in which case you will have just placed a huge bowl of yellow festive rice on the centre of the table and will be ready to surround it with *at least* as many extra separate dishes as there are guests. One doesn't prepare *rijstafel* for a romantic tête-a-tête. My first experience of *rijstafel* was when I was one of three guests at an Indonesian restaurant where 13 dishes were presented in addition to the rice. For a party of six, plan on yellow rice plus about a dozen or more selections which can include soup and prawn crackers.

The second time I had *rijstafel* was on the island of Ambon. I'd approached a bank to change money. It was closed but the bank manager heard me banging on the door, opened it and, during the exchange, invited me to his home where his charming wife offered me coffee and gifts of Indonesian batik fabrics and shirts. I wanted to reciprocate. 'Let me take you to lunch,' I cried, embarrassed by such spontaneous generosity. My host had a home telephone (unused then in Ambon, which is not on the usual tourist trail). He called a restaurant and 20 minutes later we sat at a table with his wife and three small children. The dishes kept coming, on and on, until there were about 20 in total. Despite my offer, my host insisted that he should pay as I was a guest in his country.

Daily food in
INDONESIA

Hospitality is integral to Indonesian culture, even to those who have little or nothing.) If you visit Indonesia, please give back something to those who welcome you so warmly.

A *rijstafel* is a balanced combination of many dishes and yellow rice. Dishes may include satay, a soup, appetisers (maybe meatballs and/or Indonesian spring rolls), at least one vegetable dish, one of fish, a curry, a salad, a sambal, and desserts such as banana fritters and fresh fruit. An egg curry is particularly

appropriate and provides a tasty contrast in a *rijstafel*. To make an egg curry use any curry base in this book and allocate at least one boiled, shelled egg per person. Add a couple more for those who would like seconds. It's advisable to prepare a curry a day or two in advance. Store it covered in the refrigerator then reheat it after the flavours have blended and matured.

No special tools are required to prepare Indonesian food in a reasonably well-equipped western kitchen, but a Chinese wok, and a

mortar and pestle or food processor for grinding spices are time-savers. Fresh chillies are integral to many Indonesian dishes. Wear plastic disposable gloves when preparing chillies and keep your hands away from your eyes and face as the burning sting is unbearable.

With food serve light beer, fruit juice, weak, unsweetened Chinese tea (which Indonesians take solely with their meals) or soft drinks. If authenticity isn't essential, a mild, dry, inexpensive white wine would be appropriate. Indonesian food flavours are so strong that they diminish the quality of a top wine. Serve water at the table to cool palates stimulated by spicy dishes.

An Indonesian family meal may include rice and up to four dishes. However many Indonesian families exist on rice with a sambal or curry

sauce and as many vegetables as can be found. Butter and cheese are not served. Beef is served if it is available – every bit of the cow is used; not just the meat. Do be sensitive to any Muslim guests' beliefs.

Do not include a pork dish if any guests are Muslims for although they could avoid eating it, many Muslims would consider it an insult that the cook has even considered preparing a pork dish. Some Muslims are so strict that if they believe pork has been previously cooked in a pot or pan they will not eat even the non-pork dishes cooked in that pan.

If you are on holiday in Indonesia and you are invited to dinner at the home of a local Indonesian, it is good form to bring a small gift such as chocolates or souvenirs from home, or sweets for the children. Wear neat, casual dress, not a t-shirt nor a sarong over a swimsuit. The hostess will be dressed in her best and may place her hands together, as if in Christian prayer, and bow her head in greeting. It would be polite for you to do the same.

It is quite polite in Indonesia to arrive at a private dinner party at least 10 minutes late. Usually, this is so that the hostess has had time to dress and look as radiant as possible after spending so much time preparing the meal. Traditional Indonesian families refrain from conversing during the meal; talk is reserved for afterwards. Guests should take a small serve at first because the hosts' expectations are that guests will enjoy the meal and want more. It is offensive to the cook for a guest to request extra condiments or sauces as the dishes should be perfectly flavoured and not require any extra seasoning. You should never eat with or pass something with your left hand, as this is considered unclean. Use the fingertips of your right hand to eat, which is actually quite an art. If each table place is set with a soup bowl, plate, fork and spoon, do use them. Dessert and/or fruit are served after the main repast and an extra plate is usually provided for this.

The diversity of food and styles in Indonesia is truly amazing. This selection of recipes is just a small taste of what the country has to offer. 'Selamat masak dan selamat makan!' (Happy cooking and happy eating!)

Kerry Kenihan

starters

Tempt your APPETITE

When wandering around Indonesia's street stalls, it is possible to eat a full and satisfying meal comprising completely of 'starters' which are supplied by hawkers at their *warungs* or little makeshift places. The *warungs* may be nothing more than plastic sheets over a tiny area, protecting pots and stoves from tropical rain. Diners wait while the food is cooked freshly before them. When the food is ready the diners sit on a wooden stool beside the *warung* to eat.

As in China, Vietnam, Malaysia, Thailand and Cambodia, and indeed the whole of Asia, street food is cheap and tasty. The atmosphere is particularly exciting at night when a whole food culture emerges. Families and friends gather together, chatting, picking, listening to any background music and getting up from chairs or mats for more appetisers if hunger pangs still gnaw.

In your own home, the environment will tend to be more formal as you present one or several of the following dishes to tantalise your guests with the tastes of Indonesia. That is unless you set your dinner party date for an evening by the barbecue outdoors. Spring rolls, fritters, wontons, satays, morsels of chicken and fish cakes can comprise a whole meal when served with vegetables, the staple ingredient of rice and a salad.

We suggest that home cooks choose one or two of the following starters to welcome guests to a meal redolent with spices and smoky aromas. Then continue the banquet as casually or formally as you wish.

SPRING ROLLS (LUMPIA GORENG)

Ingredients

1 tablespoon peanut oil
2 cloves garlic, crushed
4 spring onions, sliced
350g chicken mince
1 carrot, finely sliced
2 cups Chinese cabbage, shredded
2 tablespoons sweet soy sauce (kecap manis)
50g vermicelli noodles, cooked
spring roll wrappers
oil for cooking

Spring roll sauce (saus lumpia)

1 tablespoons tamarind concentrate
1 tablespoon soy sauce
2 tablespoons water
1/2 teaspoon sambal ulek
1/2 teaspoon root ginger, grated
1/2 teaspoon palm sugar or brown sugar

Method

1. Heat oil in a wok or frying pan. Add garlic, shallots and chicken mince and stir-fry for 4–5 minutes or until mince is cooked. Add carrot, cabbage and kecap manis and stir-fry for 3–4 minutes or until cooked. Combine noodles with chicken and leave to cool.

2. Place 1 tablespoon of mixture on spring roll wrappers. Roll up and brush the ends with water..

3. Heat oil in a wok or frying pan. Cook spring rolls in oil for 1–2 minutes or until golden and crisp. Combine all sauce ingredients in a small dish and set aside.

4. Drain on paper towel and serve with *saus lumpia*.

Makes about 24

CORN FRITTERS (PERKEDEL JAGUNG)

Ingredients

400g can sweetcorn, drained
1 small red chilli, deseeded and
    finely chopped
4 green shallots, sliced
1 teaspoon ground coriander
pinch of salt
1 egg
1/4 cup rice flour
1 tablespoon plain flour
vegetable oil for cooking

Method

1. Combine corn, chilli, shallots, coriander, salt, egg and flours. Leave to stand for 30 minutes.

2. Heat oil in a wok or frying pan. Drop spoonfuls of mixture into oil and cook until golden. Serve with soy sauce.

Makes about 16

INDONESIAN BEEF CROQUETTES (PERKEDEL DAGING) (opposite)

Ingredients

Pancakes

1¹/₂ cups flour

2 eggs, separated

2 cups water

pinch of salt

peanut oil for cooking

1 cup breadcrumbs

Filling

1 tablespoons peanut oil

1 brown onion, finely chopped

2 cloves garlic, crushed

400g beef mince

1–2 teaspoons chilli powder

1 tablespoon sweet soy sauce (kecap manis)

2 cups cabbage, finely shredded

Method

1. Whisk together flour, egg yolks, water and salt in a mixing bowl.

2. Heat a little oil in a frying pan. Cook pancakes one at a time, making them paper thin. Cook one side only.

3. For filling, heat oil in a frying pan. Add onion, garlic and beef mince and cook for 4–5 minutes or until meat is cooked. Add chilli powder, kecap manis and cabbage and cook for a further 2–3 minutes. Leave mixture to cool.

4. Place tablespoons of filling on each pancake. Fold to form an envelope. Dip pancakes in beaten egg whites and breadcrumbs.

5. Heat oil in a wok and cook pancakes for 1–2 minutes or until golden and crisp. Drain pancakes on paper towel. Serve with spring roll sauce (see page 12).

Makes about 12 pancakes

PINEAPPLE AND RUM TURKEY KEBABS (AYAM BELANDA NANAS)

Ingredients

375g turkey breast tenderloin steaks or boneless turkey breast

¹/₃ cup unsweetened pineapple juice

3 tablespoons rum

1 tablespoon brown sugar

1 tablespoon lemongrass, finely chopped or 2 teaspoons lemon peel, finely shredded

1 tablespoon olive oil

1 medium red onion, cut into thin wedges

2 nectarines, peeled, or 3 plums, pitted and cut into thick slices

1¹/₂ cups fresh or canned pineapple chunks

hot cooked rice (optional)

Method

1. Cut turkey into 2¹/₂cm cubes. Place turkey cubes in a plastic bag set in a shallow dish. For marinade, combine ¹/₃ cup pineapple juice, rum, brown sugar, lemongrass or lemon peel, and oil. Pour marinade over turkey; close bag. Marinate in refrigerator for 4–24 hours, turning bag occasionally.

2. Drain turkey, reserving marinade. In a small saucepan bring marinade to boil. Remove from heat. On four 30cm skewers thread alternately turkey and onion. Grill kebabs on the rack of an uncovered grill on medium heat for 12–14 minutes or until turkey is cooked but still tender, turning once and brushing occasionally with marinade.

3. Meanwhile, on four 30cm kebab skewers alternately thread nectarines or plums and pineapple chunks. Place on grill rack next to turkey kebabs for the last 5 minutes of grilling, turning and brushing once with marinade. Serve turkey and fruit kebabs with rice, if desired.

Serves 4

Indonesian

beef croquettes

CRISPY SEAFOOD WONTONS (PANGSIT GORENG)

Ingredients

100g peeled green prawns

200g fish fillets, chopped

1 clove garlic, crushed

2 green shallots, sliced

2 teaspoon soy sauce

1 egg

1 packet wonton skins

peanut oil for cooking

Wonton sauce

2 tablespoons soy sauce

2 tablespoons water

1 clove garlic, crushed

$1/2$ teaspoon root ginger, grated

$1/2$ teaspoon palm sugar or brown sugar

Method

1. Combine prawns, fish, garlic, shallots, soy sauce and egg in a food processor. Process mixture until smooth.

2. Place spoonfuls of mixture in the centre of each wonton skin. Brush the edges with a little water. Fold skin in half to form a triangle and press edges lightly to seal.

3. Combine ingredients for sauce in a small dish and set aside. Heat oil in a wok and cook wonton for 1–2 minutes or until golden and crisp. Serve with wonton sauce.

Makes about 30

CHICKEN SATAY (SATE AYAM)

Ingredients

12 bamboo skewers

500g chicken thigh fillets, diced
   (beef, lamb and pork can also be used)

2 tablespoons peanut oil

2 tablespoons sweet soy sauce (kecap manis)

1 tablespoon soy sauce

1 clove garlic, crushed

Method

1. Soak bamboo skewers in cold water for 15–20 minutes.

2. Thread diced chicken onto bamboo skewers. Place chicken in a large dish. Combine peanut oil, kecap manis, soy sauce and garlic. Pour marinade over chicken and leave to marinate in the refrigerator for 1–2 hours.

3. Cook satays on a barbecue for 10–15 minutes or until cooked.

4. Serve with peanut sauce (see page 77).

Makes about 12

SPICY MEATBALLS (REMPAH DAGING)

Ingredients

2 French shallots, chopped

2 cloves garlic, chopped

2 teaspoons cumin seeds

1 teaspoon ground coriander

500g beef mince

$1/2$ cup fresh breadcrumbs

1 egg yolk

2 teaspoons sambal ulek

1 tablespoon soy sauce

$1/4$ cup peanut oil

Method

1. Crush or pound together shallots, garlic, cumin seeds, and coriander in a mortar with pestle or small food processor.

2. Combine mixture with beef, breadcrumbs, egg yolk, sambal ulek and soy sauce. Shape mixture into small walnut-sized balls.

3. Heat oil in a large frying pan. Fry meatballs for 5–6 minutes or until golden. Serve meatballs with wedges of lime and/or sweet chilli sauce.

Makes about 20

SPICY FISH FRITTERS (PERKEDEL IKAN)

Ingredients

4 green shallots, sliced

2 cloves garlic, chopped

2 teaspoons root ginger, chopped

500g boneless fish fillets

1 tablespoon soy sauce

2 teaspoons sweet soy sauce (kecap manis)

1 egg

1 tablespoon cornflour

peanut oil for cooking

Dipping sauce

1 tablespoon sweet soy sauce

2 tablespoons soy sauce

1/2 teaspoon sambal oelek

Method

1. Combine shallots, garlic, ginger, fish, soy sauce, kecap manis, egg and cornflour in a food processor. Process until mixture comes together and is smooth.

2. Using wet hands shape mixture into small patties. (Mixture tends to be wet.) Cover with plastic wrap and let stand for 30 minutes to 1 hour in the refrigerator.

3. Heat oil in a non-stick frying pan or wok. Cook patties for 1–2 minutes each side or until golden.

4. Combine ingredients for dipping sauce in a small dish. Serve fritters with dipping sauce.

Makes about 16

SPICED CHICKEN DRUMETTES (AYAM GORENG)

Ingredients

oil for greasing

$^1/_2$ cup cornflour

2 teaspoons ground black pepper

$^1/_2$ teaspoon salt

1 teaspoon ground coriander

1 teaspoon ground cumin

$^1/_2$ teaspoon ground chilli powder

1 kg chicken drumettes

Method

1. Preheat oven to 210°C. Lightly grease or spray a non-stick baking tray with oil.

2. Combine cornflour, pepper, salt, coriander, cumin and chilli powder in a mixing bowl. Toss chicken in spice mixture to coat.

3. Place chicken on baking tray, spray lightly with oil and bake for 20–25 minutes or until golden and crisp. Serve with *sambal kecap* (see page 76) or light soy sauce.

Makes about 12

chicken

Out for a DUCK

Chicken and duck are the least expensive meats available in Indonesia, so Indonesians have drawn on all sorts of foreign-influenced recipes to make poultry presentable and tasty.

In Indonesia there are always a few chickens wandering around village houses, no matter how poor the household. Ducks are a bit more hard to obtain, but any of the following recipes can be prepared with duck if you happen to have bought one. Just allow a little more cooking time for duck.

Indonesians fry, sauté, grill, stew or oven-bake chicken as enthusiastically as we do in the West but the taste sensations differ with the cooking traditions from Java, Bali and Jakarta – and their wonderful spices. Whether in a curry or in coconut milk, or cooked Chinese-style with soy sauce, chicken is tasty, cheap and chock-a-block full of goodness, particularly if the skin is removed. *Ayam goreng* (fried chicken) is a national dish and is fairly easy to prepare.

If you are pushed for preparation time, pick up a barbecued chicken from your nearest outlet and substitute it in the following recipes.

Ideally prepare your dishes in advance and refrigerate overnight before reheating and serving. The spicy flavours will be even tastier.

JAVANESE CURRIED CHICKEN (AYAM JAWA)

Ingredients

2 tablespoons vegetable oil
4 chicken thighs
1 onion, chopped
3 cloves garlic, crushed
1 stick lemongrass, finely chopped
1 teaspoon root ginger, grated
1 teaspoon ground coriander
1 teaspoon ground turmeric
$1/2$ teaspoon ground cumin
1 cup coconut milk
6 curry leaves
$1/2$ cup coriander leaves

Method

1. Heat oil in a frying pan. Add chicken and cook for 4–5 minutes or until golden. Add onion, garlic, lemongrass and ginger. Cook until onion is soft. Add coriander, turmeric and cumin and cook until aromatic.

2. Add coconut milk and curry leaves and simmer uncovered for 15–20 minutes or until sauce has thickened. Stir through coriander leaves. Serve with *nasi putih* (see page 56).

Serves 4

SPICY CHICKEN SOUP (SOTO AYAM)

Ingredients

1 1/2 kg whole chicken

2 teaspoons salt

2 tablespoons chicken stock powder

100g vermicelli noodles

1 tablespoon peanut oil

2 cloves garlic, crushed

2 teaspoons root ginger, grated

1 stalk lemongrass, white part finely
   chopped and top part tied in a knot

1 teaspoon ground turmeric

2 teaspoons ground coriander

2 lime leaves, finely sliced

juice of 1 lime

wedges of lime to serve

Garnishes

4 green shallots, sliced

1 cup bean sprouts, trimmed

2 hard boiled eggs, quartered

2 potatoes, cooked and sliced

Method

1. Place chicken in a large saucepan. Cover with water, add salt and bring to the boil. Reduce heat, cover and simmer for 30–35 minutes or until chicken is cooked. Remove chicken and strain liquid, reserving 6 cups. Stir in chicken stock powder. Remove skin and bones from chicken and shred chicken.

2. Cook noodles according to packet directions. Drain and set aside.

3. Heat oil in a large saucepan. Add garlic, ginger and lemongrass and cook for 1–2 minutes. Add turmeric and coriander and cook until aromatic.

4. Add reserved stock, chicken and lime leaves. Simmer for 10 minutes. Add lime juice just before serving.

5. Place noodles in serving bowls. Spoon chicken soup over noodles and top with garnishes. Serve with wedges of lime, *sambal kecap* or *sambal cuka* (see page 76).

Serves 4

JAVANESE CHICKEN AND VEGETABLES (AYAM JAWA SAYUR)

Ingredients

2 tablespoons peanut oil

500g chicken thigh fillets

3 French shallots, sliced

2 cloves garlic, crushed

2 teaspoons root ginger, grated

1 teaspoon ground turmeric

1 teaspoon ground coriander

1 teaspoon ground cumin

1 teaspoon galangal powder

1 cup coconut milk

3/4 cup chicken stock

2 teaspoons sambal ulek

1 stalk lemongrass, bruised

2 salam leaves

1 carrot, sliced

2 potatoes, diced

150g green beans, sliced

Method

1. Heat oil in a large saucepan. Add chicken and cook for 4–5 minutes or until golden. Add shallots, garlic and ginger. Cook until shallots are soft. Add turmeric, coriander, cumin and galangal powder. Cook until aromatic.

2. Add coconut milk, chicken stock, sambal ulek. lemongrass and salam leaves. Bring to the boil. Add vegetables and cook for 10–15 minutes or until vegetables are tender. Serve with *nasi putih* (see page 56).

Serves 4

CHICKEN IN COCONUT MILK (OPOR AYAM)

Ingredients

2 tablespoons peanut oil

8 small chicken pieces

2 onions, sliced

2 teaspoons ground coriander

1 teaspoon ground cumin

1/2 teaspoon galangal powder

1 1/2 cups coconut cream

1 1/2 cups coconut milk

4 kaffir lime leaves, thinly sliced

Paste

2 cloves garlic

2 teaspoons root ginger, chopped

1 teaspoon terasi

3 candle nuts

1–2 small red chillis, deseeded

1/2 teaspoon salt

Method

1. Crush or pound paste ingredients in a mortar with pestle or a food processor.

2. Heat oil in a large saucepan. Add chicken and cook for 4–5 minutes or until golden. Remove chicken and set aside.

3. Add onions and cook for 3–4 minutes or until brown. Add paste and cook for 1–2 minutes. Add coriander, cumin and galangal powder and cook until aromatic.

4. Add coconut cream, coconut milk, lime leaves and chicken. Bring to the boil, reduce heat and simmer for 20–30 minutes or until chicken is tender and sauce has reduced. Serve with *nasi putih* (see page 56).

Serves 4

ROAST SPICED CHICKEN (AYAM PANGGANG PEDIS)

(opposite)

Ingredients

2 tablespoons margarine

2 cloves garlic, crushed

2 tablespoons sweet soy sauce (kecap manis)

2 tablespoons tamarind concentrate

2–3 teaspoons sambal ulek

1 1/2 kg chicken, cleaned

wedges of lime to serve

Method

1. Preheat oven to 200°C.

2. Heat margarine in a small saucepan. Add garlic and cook for 1–2 minutes. Add kecap manis, tamarind and sambal ulek. Bring to the boil. Remove from heat and brush over chicken.

3. Place chicken on a rack over a baking tray. Cover lightly with foil and bake in preheated oven for 30 minutes. Remove foil, baste chicken and bake for a further 20–30 minutes or until cooked.

4. Cut chicken into pieces and serve with lime wedges.

Serve 4

INDONESIAN CURRY (KARI INDONESIA)

Ingredients

1 tablespoon fresh ginger, grated

1 teaspoon turmeric

1 teaspoon salt

1 teaspoon sugar

1 1/2–2 kg chicken, cut into pieces

4 teaspoons vegetable oil

2 medium onions, cut into very thin wedges

1 bay leaf

400g can unsweetened coconut milk

1 1/2 kaffir lime leaves or 1 teaspoon grated lime peel

1 tablespoon chopped fresh coriander

cooked rice and soy sauce to serve

Curry paste

2 medium onions, cut into chunks

2 large garlic cloves

2 tablespoons water

2 teaspoons Madras curry powder

1 1/2 teaspoon coriander

1/2 teaspoon cinnamon

1/2 teaspoon ground red pepper

Garnish

coriander leaves, sliced spring onions, peanuts, sliced hot fresh chillies.

Method

1. Combine ginger, turmeric, salt, and sugar in a bowl; add chicken and toss well to coat. Cover and marinate chicken in the refrigerator 1–24 hours.

2. Heat 2 teaspoons of oil in a deep 30 cm skillet over medium-high heat. Add onion wedges and bay leaf and cook for 8 minutes until browned. Transfer to plate using a slotted spoon. Set aside.

3. Meanwhile, for curry paste, purée onion chunks, garlic, water, curry powder, coriander, cinnamon and red pepper in blender until smooth, scraping sides with rubber spatula if necessary.

4. Heat remaining 2 teaspoons oil in same skillet over medium-high heat; add curry paste and cook for 4–5 minutes, stirring occasionally, until thickened. Add chicken and coat with paste. Cover and simmer for 10 minutes. Stir in coconut milk, browned onions and lime leaves. Simmer uncovered for 20 minutes more until chicken is cooked through. Remove bay leaf. Divide chicken and sauce among 5 serving plates. Sprinkle with chopped coriander. Serve with rice, soy sauce and other garnishes, if desired.

Serves 5

roast spiced chicken

CRISPY FRIED DUCK (BEBEK GORENG)

Ingredients

2 tablespoons soy sauce

1 tablespoon tamarind concentrate

1 tablespoon peanut oil

1 teaspoon root ginger, grated

1 clove garlic, crushed

1 teaspoon ground coriander

4 duck breasts

$^1/_4$ cup peanut oil for cooking

salad greens to serve

Method

1. Preheat oven to 200°C.

2. Combine soy sauce, tamarind, oil, ginger, garlic and coriander to make a marinade. Pour marinade over duck and leave to marinate in the refrigerator for 2–3 hours.

3. Heat oil in a frying pan. Add duck and cook for 1–2 minutes or until golden and crisp. Place duck on a rack over a baking tray and cook for 15–18 minutes. Slice duck and serve with salad greens.

Serves 4

GRILLED CHICKEN (AYAM PANGGANG)

Ingredients

2 tablespoons peanut oil

1/3 cup soy sauce

2 tablespoons lime juice

2 tablespoons lime zest

2 teaspoons sambal ulek

2 cloves garlic, crushed

1 tablespoon palm sugar or brown sugar

8 chicken thigh fillets, trimmed

cooked rice and green vegetables to serve

Method

1. Combine oil, soy sauce, lime juice, lime zest, sambal ulek, garlic and sugar. Place chicken in dish. Pour marinade over and leave to marinate in the refrigerator for 2–3 hours.

2. Cook chicken on a barbecue plate for 10–15 minutes, occasionally basting. Serve with cooked rice, green vegetables and sweet chilli sauce (on the side).

Serves 4–6

CHICKEN AND CORN SOUP (SOP AYAM JAGUNG)

Ingredients

2 teaspoons peanut oil, extra

6 cups chicken stock

3 cups shredded cooked chicken

400g can sweetcorn kernels, drained

2 tablespoons sweet soy sauce

1–2 teaspoons sambal ulek

2 cups shredded English or Chinese spinach,
   washed and drained

salt to taste

Paste

2 French shallots, chopped

2 cloves garlic

2 candle nuts

1 teaspoon terasi

2 teaspoons peanut oil

Method

1. Crush or pound paste ingredients in a mortar with pestle or in a small food processor.

2. Heat oil in a large saucepan. Add paste and cook for 1–2 minutes. Add stock, chicken, sweetcorn, kecap manis and sambal ulek. Bring to the boil and simmer over low heat for 5–10 minutes.

3. Add spinach and cook for 1–2 minutes. Season with salt. Serve into 4 individual soup bowls.

Serves 4

BALINESE-STYLE FRIED CHICKEN (AYAM BALI)

Ingredients

¹/₄ cup peanut oil

8 small chicken pieces

³/₄–1 cup coconut milk

2 teaspoons sweet soy sauce (kecap manis)

2 tablespoons lime juice

2 tablespoons lime zest

1 long green chilli, deseeded and sliced

cook rice to serve

Paste

3 French shallots

2 cloves garlic

2 teaspoons root ginger, chopped

4 medium red chillies, deseeded and chopped

3 candle nuts

2 teaspoons sweet soy sauce (kecap manis)

Method

1. Crush or pound paste ingredients, except for kecap manis, in a mortar with pestle or in a food processor. Add kecap manis and stir to combine.

2. Heat oil in a wok or frying pan. Add chicken in two batches and cook until golden.

3. Remove chicken and drain on paper towel. Pour off excess oil in pan.

4. Cook paste for 1–2 minutes. Add coconut milk, kecap manis, lemon juice zest, chilli and chicken. Simmer for 25–30 minutes or until chicken is tender. Serve with cooked long grain rice and green beans.

Serves 4

MARINATED CHICKEN WITH SNOW PEAS (AYAM DIASINKAN DENGAN KACANG KAPRI)

Ingredients

2 cloves garlic, crushed

2 teaspoons root ginger, grated

1 lemongrass stalk, finely chopped

2 tablespoons soy sauce

1 teaspoon sambal ulek

1 tablespoons sweet soy sauce (kecap manis)

2 teaspoons sesame oil

500g chicken thigh fillets, thinly sliced

1 tablespoons peanut oil

150g snow peas, trimmed and halved

230g can bamboo shoots, drained

Method

1 Combine garlic, ginger, lemongrass, soy sauce, sambal ulek, kecap manis and sesame oil in a shallow dish to make marinade. Add chicken and coat well in marinade. Leave to marinate for 1–2 hours.

2 Heat oil in a wok or frying pan. Add chicken (reserving marinade) and stir-fry for 4–5 minutes or until golden. Add marinade, snow peas and bamboo shoots and stir-fry for 2–3 minutes or until snow peas are cooked. Add a little water if the sauce becomes too thick. Serve directly from the wok. Have boiled rice available on the side.

Serves 4

meat

Tough it OUT

Let's be frank; meat in Indonesia is not always the best. Beef usually comes from the water buffalo and it tends to be tough so Indonesians tend to boil or deep-fry it to tenderise it. These beef recipes have been adapted to allow for the availability of tender beef.

Indonesians regard beef as food with which to celebrate a special occasion. Beef is expensive and not usually part of the daily fare. Pork, on the other hand, is a big winner in Bali where it is popular with Hindus and Christians. Never serve a Muslim pork as it is against their religion to eat it.

Meat is relatively and of higher quality in the West than it is in Indonesia so you can go ahead with enthusiasm in preparing the following dishes. These dishes can be served with rice or noodles and vegetables to make a satisfying family meal. Otherwise one dish could make up part of your Indonesian dinner party with exciting Indonesian flavours.

DICED SPICY BEEF (EMPAL DAGING)

Ingredients

750g beef, thinly sliced and diced

2 tablespoons peanut oil

1 bunch snake beans, trimmed and cut into 5cm pieces.

$1/2$ cup water

Paste

1 teaspoon coriander seeds

3 cloves garlic, chopped

2 teaspoons galangal, chopped

1 teaspoon palm sugar or brown sugar

2 tablespoons tamarind concentrate

$1/4$ cup soy sauce

Garnish

toasted desiccated coconut

Method

1. Crush or pound the dry paste ingredients in a mortar and pestle or food processor. Crush until a paste has formed. Add tamarind and soy sauce.

2. Marinate beef in paste for 1–2 hours in the refrigerator.

3. Heat oil in a wok. Add beef and stir-fry for 4–5 minutes. Add beans and cook for 3–4 minutes or until beans are tender. Add a little water if too thick. Garnish with toasted coconut. Serve with boiled rice on the side.

Serves 4

DRY-FRIED BEEF CURRY (RENDANG DAGING)

Ingredients

1/4 cup desiccated coconut

1 1/2 tablespoons vegetable oil

1 kg beef, diced

2 cups coconut milk

2 salam leaves

1 stalk lemongrass, white part chopped and the top tied in a knot

Paste

3 French shallots, chopped

6–8 medium red chillies, deseeded and chopped

2 teaspoons root ginger, chopped

3 cloves garlic, chopped

1/2 teaspoon galangal powder

1 teaspoon ground turmeric

Method

1. Crush or pound paste ingredients in a mortar with pestle or food processor. (Add 2 teaspoons peanut oil if using a food processor).

2. Dry-fry desiccated coconut in a frying pan until golden.

3. Heat 1 tablespoon oil in a large saucepan. Add half the beef and stir-fry 2–3 minutes or until beef is brown. Remove and set aside. Add remaining oil and beef and stir-fry for a further 2–3 minutes. Remove and set aside. Add paste and stir-fry for 1 minute.

4. Add coconut milk, salam leaves, lemongrass stalk and beef. Bring to the boil. Reduce heat and simmer uncovered for 1 1/2 hours and or until liquid has evaporated and beef is tender. Serve with boiled rice on the side.

Serves 4

PORK IN SOY SAUCE (BABI KECAP)

Ingredients

1 tablespoon peanut oil

500g pork fillet, sliced

1 onion, sliced

3 cloves garlic, crushed

1 teaspoon root ginger, grated

1/4 cup sweet soy sauce (kecap manis)

2 tablespoons water

4 green shallots, sliced

Method

1. Heat oil in a wok. Add pork and stir-fry for 5–6 minutes or until golden. Add onions and garlic and stir-fry for 2–3 minutes. Add ginger, kecap manis, water and green shallots and cook for 2–3 minutes. Serve with side bowls of boiled rice.

Serves 4

INDONESIAN PORK SPARE RIBS (BABI TULANG CIN) (opposite)

Ingredients

750g pork spare ribs

1 1/2 tablespoons peanut oil

1 teaspoon ground coriander

1/2 teaspoon ground cumin

1/2 teaspoon ground pepper

2 tablespoons soy sauce

1 tablespoon tamarind concentrate

1 teaspoon brown sugar

1/4 cup water

Paste

2 French shallots, chopped

2 cloves garlic

2 teaspoons root ginger, chopped

Method

1. Crush or pound paste ingredients in a mortar with pestle or in a small food processor.

2. Chop spare ribs in half. Heat 1 tablespoon oil in a wok or frying pan. Add spare ribs and stir-fry for 2–3 minutes or until ribs are golden and crisp. Remove and set aside.

3. Heat remaining oil and add paste. Stir-fry for 1 minute. Add coriander, cumin, pepper, soy sauce, tamarind and sugar. Return ribs to sauce and simmer covered for 10 minutes or until ribs are cooked through. Add a little water if sauce becomes too thick. Serve with chinese greens and side bowl of rice.

Serves 4

BALINESE PORK (BABI BALI)

Ingredients

1 tablespoon peanut oil

750g pork loin or fillet pork, diced

1/4 cup sweet soy sauce

1 tablespoon lime juice

1–1 1/2 cups water

Paste

3 small red chillies, deseeded and chopped

2 French shallots, chopped

2 cloves garlic, chopped

2 teaspoons root ginger, chopped

1 teaspoon terasi

2 teaspoons peanut oil

Method

1. Crush or pound paste ingredients in a mortar with pestle or food processor.

2. Heat remaining oil in a saucepan and stir-fry paste for 1–2 minutes. Add pork and stir-fry for 4–5 minutes. Add kecap manis, lime juice and water. Cover saucepan and simmer for 1 hour. Serve with side bowls of boiled rice.

Serves 4

BEEF LIVER IN COCONUT MILK (KALIO HATI)

Ingredients

600g beef liver, well trimmed, sliced and cut into 2cm squares

3 cups coconut milk

1 teaspoon salt

Paste

8 French shallots, peeled and sliced

3 cloves garlic, peeled and sliced

14 bird's eye chillies, sliced

1cm galangal, peeled and sliced

1cm fresh turmeric, peeled and sliced

1cm piece of root ginger, peeled and sliced

2 tablespoons oil

1 lemongrass, bruised

2 kaffir lime leaves

Method

1. Prepare the paste by grinding all ingredients except oil, lemongrass and lime leaves. Heat oil in a wok and fry the paste together with lemongrass and lime leaves for 2–3 minutes.

2. Add liver and sauté for 2 minutes. Add coconut milk and salt and simmer, uncovered, until liver is tender and sauce has thickened. Serve with side bowls of boiled rice.

Serves 4

Indonesian pork spare ribs

LAMB COOKED WITH TOMATOES (KAMBING MASAK TOMATO)

Ingredients

1 tablespoon vegetable oil

4 lamb chops, trimmed

1 onion, sliced

420g can diced tomatoes

1/2 cup beef stock

1 stalk lemongrass, bruised

2 potatoes, peeled and diced

Paste

2 cloves garlic, chopped

4 medium chillies, deseeded and chopped

pinch of salt

Method

1. Crush or pound paste ingredients in a mortar with pestle or a food processor.

2. Heat oil in a large saucepan. Add chops and cook for 2–3 minutes on each side or until brown. Remove and set aside. Add onion and cook for 2–3 minutes.

3. Add paste to saucepan and cook for 1–2 minutes. Add tomatoes, stock, lemongrass, potatoes and chops. Cover and simmer for 30–40 minutes or until chops are tender and sauce has reduced. Serve with side bowls of boiled rice.

Serves 4

BARBECUED LAMB CUTLETS (KAMBING PANGGANG)

Ingredients

2 tablespoons peanut oil

¼ cup lemon juice

1 tablespoon soy sauce

2 cloves garlic, crushed

1 teaspoon ground coriander

1 teaspoon ground cumin

8 lamb cutlets

Method

1. Combine oil, lemon juice, soy sauce, garlic, coriander and cumin to make marinade. Place lamb cutlets in a dish. Pour marinade over and marinate in the refrigerator for 2–3 hours.

2. Cook lamb cutlets on a barbecue plate for 8–10 minutes, occasionally basting.

3. Serve with *nasi goreng* (see page 53) and peanut sauce (see page 77).

Serves 4

BEEF IN TAMARIND (DAGING ASAM)

Ingredients

1 tablespoon peanut oil, extra

750g rump beef, diced

3 green shallots, sliced

2 medium red chillies, deseeded and sliced

1 tablespoon sweet soy sauce (kecap manis)

1 tablespoon tamarind concentrate

$^1/_2$–$^3/_4$ cup beef stock

1 eggplant, diced

Paste

2 French shallots, chopped

2 cloves garlic, chopped

$^1/_2$ teaspoon terasi

2 teaspoons peanut oil

Method

1. Crush or pound paste ingredients in a mortar with pestle or a food processor.

2. Heat oil in a wok or saucepan. Add beef and stir-fry for 3–4 minutes or until brown. Add paste and shallots and stir-fry for 2–3 minutes. Add chillies, kecap manis, tamarind and stock. Reduce heat, cover and simmer for 10 minutes. Add eggplant and cook for a further 5–6 minutes or until beef is tender and sauce has reduced. Stir through green shallots and serve with side bowls of boiled rice.

Serves 4

seafood

Spicy hot or COCONUT CREAM

Pontianak and Samarinda in Kalimantan have enormous river prawns while Jayapura offers Indonesia's best selection of barbecued fish. While the fish and seafood recipes to follow rely on fresh produce, many Indonesians rely on dried fish because of the lack of refrigeration in many communities.

Fresh fish is prepared in so many ways. It may be grilled or barbecued over charcoals, wrapped in a banana leaf (or foil in your home kitchen) and baked, be it tuna, carp, mullet, bream or bass. Shellfish comes in the form of garlic-and-butter-sauced prawns, which also make sensational satays, and West Javanese spiced prawn balls. Also from Java comes *otak-otak*. In this dish, cooked prawns are combined with double the amount of firm fish fillets along with chillies, spring onions, garlic, lemongrass, coriander and unsweetened coconut milk. This is divided among banana leaves (or foil) and baked, steamed or grilled. The result is a delicious fish paté.

Alternatively, one can make fish foil parcels from fish fillets, spices and coconut cream and quickly barbecue them over hot coals. Fish in soy sauce is popular in Sumatra. If you visit Ujung Pandang, the capital of Sulawesi, you'll find a huge variety of barbecued fish, including squid, prepared by the seafaring Bugis people at their numerous stalls.

Fish fillets fried then topped with a lime juice, soy sauce, coconut cream and vinegar sauce, are another delicious surprise for Westerners. Squid is popular in curry and is also fiery when cooked with dried chillies and shrimp paste. Other delicacies include lobster, crab and anchovies.

SAMBAL FRIED PRAWNS (UDANG GORENG)

Ingredients

1 tablespoon vegetable oil
24 green prawns, heads and shells removed

Paste

3 cloves garlic, chopped
3 medium chillies, deseeded and chopped
3 teaspoons root ginger, chopped
1 stalk lemongrass, chopped
1 teaspoon ground coriander
pinch of salt
2 teaspoons vegetable oil

Method

1. Crush or pound paste ingredients in a mortar with pestle or a food processor.

2. Heat remaining oil in a wok or frying pan. Add prawns and paste, and stir-fry for 3–4 minutes or until cooked.

3. Serve prawns with *nasi goreng* (see page 53) or *nasi putih* (see page 56).

Serves 4

BAKED FISH WITH SPICY SOY SAUCE (IKAN KECAP)

Ingredients

800g–1 kg whole snapper
2 teaspoons peanut oil
1 tablespoon lemon juice
pinch of salt
lemon slices

Sauce

2 teaspoons peanut oil
2 cloves garlic, crushed
2 teaspoons root ginger, grated
1 small red chilli, deseeded and sliced
4 green shallots, sliced
2 tablespoons soy sauce
1 tablespoon sweet soy sauce (kecap manis)
1/2 cup water

Method

1. Preheat oven to 200°C. Make two diagonal cuts on each side of the fish. Brush fish with oil and lemon juice. Season with salt and place slices of lemon in the fish. Wrap fish up in baking paper and aluminium foil and place on a baking tray. Bake in preheated oven for 30–40 minutes or until cooked.

2. Heat oil in a small saucepan. Add garlic, ginger, chilli and shallots and cook for 1–2 minutes. Add soy sauce, kecap manis and water and cook for 2–3 minutes.

3. When fish is cooked, transfer to a large serving dish and pour sauce over it. Serve with side bowls of boiled rice.

Serves 4

CALAMARI (CUMI-CUMI GORENG)

Ingredients

1/4 cup lemon juice

1/2 teaspoon ground turmeric

1 clove garlic, crushed

pinch of salt

500g squid

1/2 cup plain flour

oil for cooking

a sprinkle of chilli flakes and lemon or
  lime wedges to serve

Method

1. Combine lemon juice, turmeric, garlic and salt to make marinade.

2. Cut squid into rings or pieces. Place squid in a dish. Pour marinade over and marinate for 2–3 hours in the refrigerator.

3. Dip squid in flour and deep-fry in hot oil until golden and crisp.

4. Serve squid with chilli flakes and lemon or lime wedges.

Serves 4

PAN-FRIED FISH (IKAN GORENG)

Ingredients

1 tablespoon peanut oil

4 boneless fish fillets

1 cup coconut milk

1 teaspoon palm sugar or brown sugar

1 tablespoon lemon juice

4 green shallots, sliced

Paste

2 cloves garlic, chopped

2 teaspoons root ginger, chopped

1 stalk lemongrass, sliced

2 medium chillies, deseeded and sliced

2 candle nuts

1 teaspoon terasi

1 teaspoon ground coriander

2 teaspoons peanut oil

Method

1. Grind or pound paste ingredients in a mortar with pestle or a food processor. Brush paste over fish fillets.

2. Heat remaining oil in a large frying pan. Add fish fillets and cook for 1–2 minutes on each side. Add coconut milk, sugar and lemon juice and simmer for 2–3 minutes. Serve fish topped with green shallots.

Serves 4

FISH IN BANANA LEAVES (IKAN PANGGANG) (opposite)

Ingredients

8 pieces banana leaf

750g boneless white fish fillets, diced

2 French shallots, chopped

2 cloves garlic, chopped

1 tablespoon root ginger, chopped

1/4 teaspoon ground turmeric

2 teaspoons ground coriander

1/3 cup coconut milk

juice of 1 lime

salt to taste

4 medium-sized red chillies, deseeded and sliced

4 lime leaves, shredded

Method

1. Prepare banana leaves by cutting into 15 cm square pieces. Dip each leaf in a bowl of bowling water.

2. Combine fish, shallots, garlic, ginger, turmeric, coriander, coconut milk, lime juice and salt in a food processor. Process until mixture comes together.

3. Divide mixture evenly into 8 and place in the middle of each banana leaf. Top with chilli and lime leaves. Fold banana leaf over fish, flatten a little and secure ends with tooth picks.

4. Cook fish on a barbecue for 3 minutes each side or cook in a steamer for 3–4 minutes. Serve with wedges of lime.

Serves 4

PRAWNS IN HOT SAUCE (SAMBAL UDANG)

Ingredients

500g prawns

5 pods of twisted cluster beans
   (about 20 beans, optional)

2 cups coconut milk

4 potatoes, peeled and cut into wedges

1 tablespoon tamarind juice

1 teaspoon salt

Paste

5 French shallots

2 cloves garlic

5 red chillies, sliced

1/2 teaspoon terasi

2 tablespoons oil

Method

1. Peel prawns and remove intestinal tract. Open bean pods and remove beans.

2. Prepare paste by grinding or pounding all paste ingredients except oil. Heat oil and sauté spice paste until fragrant.

3. Add prawns and sauté until they change colour. Add beans and coconut milk and bring to the boil, stirring. Add potatoes and tamarind juice and simmer, uncovered, until potatoes and prawns are cooked and sauce has thickened. Season with salt and serve.

Serves 4

GRILLED FISH WITH TOMATO SAMBAL (IKAN BAKAR COLO-COLO)

Ingredients

1 whole fish, approximately 1 kg, cleaned

1/2 teaspoon salt

1 tablespoon lime juice

2 tablespoons oil

large piece of banana leaf or aluminium
   foil to wrap fish

Colo-colo sambal

3 tablespoons lime or lemon juice

2 tomatoes, cut in half and sliced

5 red chillies, seeded and sliced

4 French shallots, peeled and sliced

4 tablespoons light soy sauce

4 sprigs basil, chopped

Method

1. Season fish with salt and lime juice, then brush with oil. Wrap fish in banana leaf and place parcel directly on charcoal or under a grill. Cook until banana leaf is evenly browned and fish is done.

2. To make colo-colo sambal, combine all ingredients and mix well.

3. The sambal can be poured over the fish when serving or, as is usually the case in Indonesia, put into individual sauce bowls for each diner to add to the fish as liked.

Serves 4

SEAFOOD CURRY (KARI IKAN UDANG CUMI-CUMI)

Ingredients

1 tablespoon peanut oil

1/2 teaspoon ground turmeric

1 teaspoon ground coriander

1 cup coconut milk

1/4 cup water

2 tablespoons lime juice

2 teaspoons palm sugar or brown sugar

2 lime leaves, shredded

400g ling fillets, diced

200g green prawns, heads removed and shelled

200g squid rings

Paste

2 French shallots, chopped

2 cloves garlic, chopped

2 teaspoons root ginger, chopped

3 medium chillies, deseeded and sliced

1 lemongrass stalk, sliced

1/2 teaspoon salt

Method

1. Grind or pound paste ingredients in a mortar with pestle or in a food processor.

2. Heat oil in a wok or large frying pan. Add paste and cook for 1–2 minutes. Add turmeric and coriander and cook until aromatic. Add coconut milk, water, lime juice, palm sugar and lime leaves. Bring to the boil, add seafood and cook for 3–4 minutes or until seafood is tender. Serve seafood with noodles or rice.

Serves 4

MARINATED BARBECUE SEAFOOD (UDANG CUMI-CUMI BAKAR)

Ingredients

$^1/_4$ cup peanut oil

grated rind of 2 limes

$^1/_3$ cup lime juice

3 medium chillies, deseeded and finely chopped

3 cloves garlic, crushed

400g squid cut into pieces

16 large green prawns, shells removed

500g baby octopus, cleaned and trimmed

Method

1. Combine oil, rind, lime juice, chillies and garlic in a shallow dish. Score the inside skin of squid diagonally in both directions.

2. Thread prawns longways onto bamboo skewers and brush marinade over prawns. Add squid pieces and octopus and brush with marinade. Leave to marinate in a refrigerator for 30 minutes.

3. Cook prawns, calamari and octopus on a barbecue plate or chargrill for 5–10 minutes or until cooked. Serve with side bowls of boiled rice.

Serves 4

SAMBAL FRIED SNAPPER (SAMBAL IKAN GORENG)

Ingredients

1 teaspoon ground cumin
1 teaspoon ground coriander
rind of 1 lime, grated
2 tablespoons lime juice
salt to taste
4 small snapper
$1/3$ cup plain flour
peanut oil for cooking

Marinade

2 French shallots, chopped
2 cloves garlic, chopped
2 teaspoons root ginger, chopped
2 medium chillies, deseeded and sliced

Method

1. Grind or pound paste ingredients in a mortar with pestle, or in a food processor. Combine paste with cumin, coriander, rind, lime juice and salt to make marinade

2. Make two slits on each side of the snapper. Brush mixture over fish and marinate for 1 hour in the refrigerator. Dip fish in flour.

3. Heat oil in a wok or large frying pan. Cook fish for 2–3 minutes on each side or until crisp on the outside and cooked through. Serve with the sambals of your choice.

Serves 4

noodles
& rice

More and MORE, PLEASE

Many Indonesians, particularly the elderly, have known severe poverty. Rice, having been grown so successfully and cheaply, has often been the only sustenance for the poor. No wonder rice is the traditional focus of every meal.

The Indonesians are masters of making rice interesting, even if it is only accompanied by a small amount of vegetables, fish or meat and/or sambals. The rice absorbs the palate-testing sauces which makes the dish exciting. Indonesian rice is dry; it is not as sticky as other Asian rice. The exception is glutinous rice, which is usually reserved for desserts.

The best method of cooking rice is by the absorption method or steaming, as more flavour is thus retained than when boiled. When rice is cooked in coconut milk it takes on a new flavour altogether. Left-over rice can be fried to produce *nasi goreng* which must be the world's greatest national dish to be based on left-overs. *Nasi goreng* bears little similarity to the Chinese version of fried rice.

Yellow rice and coconut rice, a feature of Balinese and Javanese cooking, are celebratory dishes at festivals or special family occasions. *Nasi kuning* (yellow rice) is a simple and sustaining dish and is the basis of *risjtafel*.

Noodles are also popular in Indonesia but are not generally eaten in conjunction with rice. So, for your own dinner party, make your choice: noodles or rice.

FRIED NOODLES (BAKMI GORENG)

Ingredients

200g dried egg noodles or thin noodles

1 tablespoon peanut oil

4 French shallots, sliced

500g chicken thigh fillets, diced

2 cloves garlic, crushed

1 carrot, peeled and finely sliced or grated

2 cups Chinese cabbage, shredded

2 tablespoons sweet soy sauce (kecap manis)

1/3 cup chicken stock

1 cup bean sprouts

4 green shallots, sliced

Method

1. Cook noodles following packet directions. Drain and set noodles aside.

2. Heat oil in a wok. Add shallots and cook until golden. Add chicken and garlic and stir-fry until just cooked. Add carrots and stir-fry for a further 2 minutes. Add cabbage, kecap manis and stock and continue to cook until cabbage is wilted.

3. Add noodles, bean sprouts and green shallots and stir-fry until heated through.

Serves 4

FRIED RICE (NASI GORENG)

Ingredients

2 cups long-grain rice, rinsed

1½ tablespoons peanut oil

2 eggs, lightly beaten

4 green shallots, finely sliced

2 cloves garlic, crushed

2 small red chillies, deseeded and finely chopped

300g chicken thigh fillets, diced

1 carrot, finely sliced or grated

2 cups shredded Chinese cabbage

100g prawns, peeled and cooked

2–3 tablespoons sweet soy sauce (kecap manis)

1 tablespoon soy sauce

Method

1. Cook rice in boiling salted water for 10–12 minutes or until cooked. Drain and rinse.

2. Heat 2 teaspoons oil in a wok. Add egg and swirl to coat the wok to form an omelette. Turn omelette and cook the other side. Remove and cut into thin strips.

3. Heat remaining oil in wok. Add green shallots, garlic and chilli and cook for 1–2 minutes. Add chicken and stir-fry for 3 minutes. Add carrot, cabbage, prawns, kecap manis and soy sauce and stir-fry until cabbage wilts.

4. Add rice to mixture and stir-fry until heated through. Serve rice with strips of omelette, fried shallots and the sambal of your choice.

Note: This dish can be served as a meal with chicken satay and garnished with a fried egg. Ingredients in rice can vary to suit your taste. If serving with meats you can omit the chicken and prawns.

Serves 6

YELLOW RICE (NASI KUNING)

Ingredients

1 tablespoon vegetable oil

1 teaspoon ground turmeric

1 teaspoon ground coriander

1/2 teaspoon ground cumin

2 cups long-grain rice, rinsed

2 cups coconut milk

1 cup water

6–8 curry leaves

1 cinnamon stick

Method

1. Heat oil in a large saucepan. Add turmeric, coriander, cumin and rice. Stir for 1 minute to coat rice and cook until aromatic.

2. Add coconut milk, water, curry leaves and cinnamon stick and bring to the boil. Reduce heat to low and cook for 10–12 minutes or until liquid is absorbed. Transfer rice to a steamer and steam rice for 12–15 minutes, stirring from time to time or until grains are light. If you don't have a steamer, continue to cook rice on the lowest heat for 5–10 minutes or until cooked. Remove curry leaves and cinnamon stick and serve immediately.

Note: This rice is traditionally served at special occasions.

Serves 4

FRAGRANT RICE (NASI GURIH)

Ingredients

1 tablespoon vegetable oil

2 cloves garlic, crushed

6 green shallots, sliced

1 teaspoon ground coriander

$^1/_2$ teaspoon galangal powder

2 cups long-grain rice, rinsed

2 cups coconut milk

$^1/_2$–1 cup water

6–8 curry leaves

Method

1. Heat oil in a large saucepan. Add garlic, green shallots, coriander, galangal powder and rice. Stir for 1 minute to coat rice and cook until aromatic.

2. Add coconut milk, water and curry leaves and bring to the boil. Reduce heat to low and cook for 10 minutes stirring from time to time or until liquid is absorbed. Transfer rice to a steamer and steam for 10–12 minutes or until grains are light. If you don't have a steamer continue to cook rice at the lowest heat for 5–10 minutes or until cooked. Remove curry leaves and serve immediately.

Serves 4

CHICKEN RICE WITH PINEAPPLE (NASI KEBULI) (opposite)

Ingredients

2 tablespoons butter or oil

500g boneless chicken, diced into 1cm cubes

3 cups chicken stock

1 teaspoon salt

2 cups long-grain rice, washed and drained

1/2 small pineapple, peeled and sliced
    and cut into small pieces and fried shallot to serve

Seasoning

13 French shallots, peeled and finely chopped

7 cloves garlic, peeled and finely chopped

2 1/2 cm piece of root ginger, peeled and chopped

1 teaspoon coriander

1/2 teaspoon white peppercorns

1/2 teaspoon cumin

a little nutmeg, freshly grated

8cm cinnamon stick

4 cardamom pods, bruised

2 cloves

1 lemongrass stalk, bruised

Method

1. Heat butter or oil in a wok or heavy saucepan. Add all seasoning ingredients and sauté for 2–3 minutes. Add chicken and continue sautéing for 3 minutes over high heat.

2. Add chicken stock and salt and simmer until chicken is tender. Strain stock and put chicken pieces aside.

3. Place rice in a rice cooker or heavy stock pot, add 2 1/2 cups of the reserved chicken stock and bring to the boil. Cover pan and simmer until rice is almost cooked and liquid is absorbed. Add diced chicken and cook over low heat until rice is thoroughly cooked.

4. Serve on a platter garnished with fried shallots and pineapple pieces.

Serves 4

CORN RICE (NASI JAGUNG)

Ingredients

1 1/2 cups rice, washed thoroughly

1 1/2 cups sweetcorn kernels cut from
    raw corn cobs, or tinned sweetcorn

Method

1. Put the rice and raw sweetcorn in a pot with 3 cups of water and bring to the boil. If using tinned sweetcorn, do not add at this stage.

2. Simmer rice and corn until water is absorbed. If using tinned sweetcorn, add now. Reduce heat to low and cook rice and corn for a further 10 minutes until rice is dry and fluffy. Serve immediately.

Serves 4

WHITE RICE (NASI PUTIH)

Ingredients

2 cups short-grain rice

2–3 cups water

1 teaspoon salt

Method

1. Combine rice, water and salt in a large saucepan. Bring to the boil. Reduce heat to very low, cover and allow to steam for 15 minutes or until rice is tender before serving.

Serves 4

chicken rice with pineapple

VEGETABLES AND NOODLES IN CURRY (KARI SAYUR)

Ingredients

2 teaspoons peanut oil

1/2 teaspoon ground turmeric

1 teaspoon ground cumin

1/2 cup coconut milk

1 cup chicken stock

2 teaspoons brown sugar

1 head broccoli, cut into florets

1/2 cauliflower, cut into florets

1 carrot, sliced

600g fresh thin noodles

Paste

1 clove garlic, chopped

1 French shallot, chopped

1 medium chilli, deseeded and chopped

2 teaspoons peanut oil

Method

1. Crush or pound paste ingredients in a mortar with pestle, or in a food processor.

2. Heat remaining oil in a saucepan. Add paste and stir-fry for 1–2 minutes. Add turmeric and cumin and stir-fry until aromatic. Add coconut milk, chicken stock, brown sugar, broccoli, cauliflower and carrot. Bring to the boil, then reduce heat. Cover and cook for 6–8 minutes or until vegetables are tender. Stir in noodles and serve.

Serves 4

vegetables

Rich from THE SOIL

If any dedicated vegetarians have reservations about being beach-bums or upmarket holiday resort guests in Bali, let this section alleviate their fears. In Bali and almost everywhere else in Indonesia, particularly in rural areas, fresh, steamed vegetables are available from roadside stalls as well as in restaurants and hotels. Vegetables are very much a part of the meal scene in Indonesia. No *rijstafel* would be authentic without vegetables. Indonesia also has an exclusive specialty; fermented soybean cake tempeh.

The island nation has its own indigenous vegetables which thrive in rich volcanic soil. The vegetable selection was broadened by European conquerors such as the Dutch who discovered that tomatoes, beans, cabbages and carrots would grow well in Indonesia. Much earlier, the Chinese had planted eggplant, cucumbers and spinach, which also thrived. Sweetcorn, bean sprouts and cauliflower are also grown. The Indonesians frequently combine vegetables and fruit and, in addition, vegetables with tofu. *Gado gado* is a national dish which includes eggs, potatoes and peanut sauce. It is somewhat time-consuming to prepare but it is rewarding and healthy for non-meat-eaters, especially if tofu is added and the vegetables are not over-cooked.

Indonesian-style vegetables can be stir-fried, fried, stuffed into pancakes, simmered in coconut milk, made into croquettes and fritters or used to give a spicy flavour to omelettes. Along with rice, at least two vegetable dishes should be served in a traditional Indonesian meal.

GREEN BEANS WITH SOY SAUCE (BUNCIS KECAP)

Ingredients

1 tablespoon peanut oil
1 teaspoon sesame oil
1 clove garlic, crushed
2 French shallots, sliced
300g green beans, trimmed and halved
2 tablespoons soy sauce
2 tablespoons water
1 cup bean sprouts, trimmed
1/3 cup roasted peanuts, chopped

Method

1. Heat oil in a wok or frying pan. Add sesame oil, garlic, shallots and beans. Stir-fry for 2–3 minutes. Add soy sauce and water and cook for 3–4 minutes or until beans are just cooked. Stir through bean sprouts and peanuts. Serve warm or cold.

Serves 4

VEGETABLES WITH PEANUT SAUCE (GADO GADO)

Ingredients

2 large potatoes, peeled and cooked

150g snake beans, blanched

2 carrots, sliced and blanched

100g beancurd, diced and deep fried

4 eggs, hard-boiled and quartered

1 cucumber, sliced

1 cup bean sprouts, trimmed

Peanut sauce (see page 77)

Method

1. Place vegetables on a large platter and serve with peanut sauce and the sambals of your choice.

Serves 4

VEGETABLES IN COCONUT MILK (SAYUR LODEH)

Ingredients

1 tablespoon peanut oil

1 onion, sliced

2 cloves garlic, crushed

1 teaspoon terasi, crushed

2 candle nuts, crushed

1 cup coconut milk

1 cup chicken stock

1 teaspoon sambal ulek

1 stalk lemongrass, bruised

1 piece broccoli, cut into florets

1/4 cauliflower, cut into florets

1 large zucchini, halved and sliced

150g green beans, sliced

Method

1. Heat oil in a large saucepan. Add onion and cook for 2–3 minutes or until soft. Add garlic, terasi and candle nuts and cook for 1 minute.

2. Add coconut milk, chicken stock, sambal ulek and lemongrass. Bring to the boil. Add broccoli and cauliflower and simmer, covered, for 4 minutes. Add zucchini and beans and continue to cook for 3–4 minutes or until vegetables are just tender.

3. Remove lemongrass and serve.

Serves 4

SPICY SNAKE BEANS (SAMBAL BUNCIS)

Ingredients

2 teaspoons peanut oil

1/2 cup chicken stock

1 stalk lemongrass, bruised

250g snake beans, trimmed

Paste

2 medium red chillies, deseeded and sliced

2 French shallots, chopped

2 teaspoons root ginger, chopped

2 teaspoons garlic, chopped

Method

1. Grind or pound paste ingredients in a mortar with pestle, or in a small food processor. If using a food processor you may need to add a little oil.

2. Heat oil in a wok or frying pan. Add paste and cook for 1–2 minutes. Add stock and lemongrass. Bring to the boil. Add beans and cook for 8–10 minutes or until beans are tender.

Note: Asian greens can be used instead of beans.

Serves 4

SPICY FRIED EGGPLANT (TERUNG GORENG)

Ingredients

2 eggplant, cut into 1cm slices

1/2 cup peanut oil

2 onions, sliced

2 cloves garlic, crushed

2 small chillies, deseeded and finely chopped

1 teaspoon ground coriander

2 tablespoons tamarind concentrate

1/4 cup water

1 teaspoon palm sugar or brown sugar

2 green shallots, sliced

Method

1. Brush eggplant slices with oil, reserving 1 tablespoon of oil. Heat a large non-stick frying pan. Add eggplants and cook 1–2 minutes on each side until golden. Remove and set aside.

2. Heat remaining oil. Add onions and cook for 4–5 minutes or until golden. Add garlic, chillies, coriander, tamarind, water and sugar. Return eggplant to pan and cook until sauce reduces. Garnish with green shallots. Serve with side bowls of boiled rice.

Serves 4

SOUR VEGETABLES (SAYUR ASAM)

Ingredients

1 tablespoon peanut oil

1 teaspoon galangal powder

1 cup chicken stock

2 tablespoons tamarind concentrate

1 teaspoon palm sugar or brown sugar

2 zucchinis, sliced

1 eggplant, diced, or 3 baby eggplants, sliced

1 cup shredded cabbage

150g green beans

Paste

2 French shallots, chopped

2 cloves garlic

2 medium chillies, deseeded and chopped

1 teaspoon terasi

Method

1. Crush or pound paste ingredients in a mortar with pestle or in a small food processor. If using a food processor you may need to add a little oil.

2. Heat oil in a wok or saucepan. Add paste and galangal powder and cook for 1 minute. Add chicken stock, tamarind and sugar. Bring to the boil, add vegetables and cook for 6–8 minutes or until vegetables are tender. Can be serve as a main or side dish.

Serves 4

FRIED BEANCURD IN SOY SAUCE (TAHU GORENG KECAP)

Ingredients

¹/₂ cup peanut oil

250g beancurd, diced

2 teaspoons peanut oil, extra

2 teaspoons root ginger, grated

2 medium-sized chillies, deseeded and sliced

¹/₄ cup soy sauce

2 tablespoons water

2 teaspoons palm sugar or brown sugar

200g snow peas, trimmed and halved

1 cup bean sprouts, trimmed

Method

1. Heat oil in a wok or frying pan. Add beancurd and cook until golden and crisp. Remove and set aside.

2. Heat extra oil and add ginger and chillies. Stir-fry for 1–2 minutes. Add soy sauce, water, sugar, beancurd and snow peas. Stir-fry for 2–3 minutes or until snow peas are tender. Stir through bean sprouts and serve.

Serves 4

SPICY FRIED TEMPEH (SAMBAL GORENG TEMPE)

Ingredients

1/2 cup peanut oil

300g tempeh, cut into thin strips

2 teaspoons peanut oil, extra

2 cloves garlic, crushed

1/2 teaspoon terasi

1 tablespoon tamarind concentrate

2 tablespoon soy sauce

1 teaspoon palm sugar or brown sugar

2 tablespoons water

2 green shallots, sliced

1 medium red chilli, deseeded and sliced

Method

1. Heat 1/2 cup oil in a wok or frying pan. Cook tempeh in batches until golden and crisp. Remove and set aside.

2. Heat extra oil, garlic and terasi and cook for 30 seconds. Add tamarind, soy sauce, sugar, water and tempeh. Cook until sauce has reduced.

3. Garnish with sliced green shallots and chillies. Can be serve as a main or side dish.

Serves 4

MIXED VEGETABLE SALAD (JUKUT URAB)

Ingredients

$1/4$ Chinese cabbage, shredded

150g snake beans, blanched and sliced

1 bunch spinach, shredded

1 cup bean sprouts, trimmed

1–2 long red chillies, deseeded and sliced

2 tablespoons shredded coconut, toasted

$1/4$ cup peanuts, toasted

Dressing

$1/4$ cup vegetable oil

2 tablespoons lime juice

1 tablespoon white vinegar

1 teaspoon sambal ulek

1 teaspoon brown sugar

Method

1. Combine cabbage, snake beans, spinach, bean sprouts, chillies, coconut and peanuts in a large serving dish.

2. Combine oil, lime juice, vinegar, sambal ulek and sugar in a jug. Pour dressing over salad and toss to combine. Can be serve as a main or side dish.

Serves 4

desserts

Fruit takes
THE CAKE

With such a plethora of delectable tropical fruits, it's natural that Indonesians serve them peeled and either whole or sliced. They also use fruit as additions to other sweet finishers such as blancmange – for example lychees and pineapple. Banana balls are regarded as a national dish in Indonesia. Other desserts made from glutinous or sticky rice – for example when combined with coconut milk and palm sugar syrup – satisfy the many Indonesians who have a sweet tooth.

In Sumatra and Java, steamed coconut pudding is a simple favourite, while rice cake, loved also in Sumatra, and Balinese sticky rice dumplings, appeal to most western tastes. Pancakes are a hit when made with shredded coconut and coconut milk. These pancakes puff up with the addition of ground unsalted peanuts, sesame seeds and baking powder. You can't go wrong with banana or pineapple fritters if presenting a dinner party on any tropical Asian theme. In Indonesia, fritter batter is made from tapioca flour, coconut milk and shredded coconut with baking powder and salt. Pancakes or crepes prepared with brown rice and plain flour, stuffed with mangoes and drizzled with coconut cream and sugar syrup are sensational.

Can you imagine a fruit salad of chopped grapefruit, orange, green apples, lemon juice and pineapple mixed with diced cucumber, dried shrimp paste, sambal ulek (traditional chilli sauce), soy sauce and sugar? Grilled for a few minutes in foil. Cakes are also baked for important celebrations.

However, as in other parts of Asia, these desserts are not often served as meal finishers but as festive food to be taken with Chinese tea and on special occasions. In addition to the fruits named above, Indonesian fresh fruit desserts include jackfruit, tangerines, papayas, rambutans, avocados, breadfruit, lychees, tangerines, mangosteens. and 40 different types of banana.

FRUIT SALAD IN SPICY LIME SYRUP (RUJAK)

Ingredients

1/2 pineapple, diced

1 mango, diced

1 papaya, diced

1 apple, cored and diced

1 cucumber, diced

12 rambutans, peeled and deseeded

Syrup

1 cup grated palm sugar or brown sugar

1/3 cup water

rind of 1 lime

2 tablespoons lime juice

1 teaspoon tamarind concentrate

1 medium-sized chilli, deseeded and finely chopped

Method

1. Combine sugar, water, rind and lime juice in a small saucepan to make the syrup. Bring to the boil and simmer over low heat for 8–10 minutes and allow to cool. Add tamarind and chilli and stir to combine.

2. Combine fruit in a serving bowl. Pour over syrup and toss before serving.

Serves 4

COCONUT PANCAKES (DADAR GULANG)

Ingredients

¹/₂ cup plain flour

1 tablespoon caster sugar

2 eggs, lightly beaten

³/₄ cup milk or coconut milk

oil spray for cooking

1 cup grated palm sugar or brown sugar

¹/₂ cup water

1 pandan leaf

1 cup shredded coconut, toasted

1 papaya, diced

Method

1. Combine flour and sugar in a mixing bowl. Add eggs and milk and whisk mixture until smooth. Add a little water if too thick.

2. Heat a frying pan. Spray with oil, then add enough mixture to make a thin pancake. Cook pancakes for 1–2 minutes on each side.

3. Combine sugar, water and pandan leaf in a saucepan. Bring to the boil and simmer over low heat, stirring stir until sugar dissolves and syrup thickens slightly.

4. Place coconut and papaya on each pancake and roll up. Serve pancakes with ice cream and drizzle with syrup.

Makes 8

FRIED BANANA (PISANG GORENG)

(opposite)

Ingredients

3/4 cup rice flour

1 teaspoon ground cinnamon

1 teaspoon caster sugar

2/3 cup water

3 bananas, peeled

vegetable oil for cooking

Method

1. Combine flour, cinnamon, sugar and water in a mixing bowl. Whisk mixture together until it makes a smooth batter.

2. Cut bananas in half lengthways and then into pieces. Dip banana pieces in batter.

3. Heat oil in a wok or frying pan, add banana and cook until golden and crisp. Serve with cream or ice cream.

Serves 4

RICE FLOUR DESSERT (BUBUR SUMSUM)

Ingredients

1 1/2 cups rice flour

6 cups water

1 teaspoon powdered white writing chalk

freshly grated coconut or
   moistened desiccated coconut

1/2 teaspoon salt

palm sugar syrup (see page 74)

Method

1. Combine flour, water and chalk, and mix well. Strain through a fine sieve into a heavy pan, preferably non-stick. Bring to the boil, then reduce heat and simmer for about 30 minutes until mixture thickens.

2. Cool to room temperature and serve topped with freshly grated coconut mixed with salt, and pour palm sugar syrup over the top.

Note: The sort of chalk used for writing on blackboards may seem a surprising ingredient, but according to Indonesian cooks, it 'adds a gentle, soft flavour'.

Serves 4

FRIED BANANA CAKES (PISANG GORENG)

Ingredients

6 medium-sized ripe bananas, peeled

1 tablespoon white sugar

1 tablespoon plain flour

oil for deep-frying

Method

1. Mash bananas finely and mix with sugar and sifted flour. Heat oil in a wok and drop in a large spoonful of batter. Cook several at one time, but do not overcrowd the wok or the temperature of the oil will be lowered. When cakes are crisp and golden-brown, drain on paper towel. Serve while still warm.

Serves 4

FRUIT IN COCONUT MILK (ES KOLAK)

Ingredients

4 cups coconut milk

4 tablespoons palm sugar syrup

pinch of salt

1 large or 2 small bananas, sliced

2 pieces of ripe jackfruit, finely diced

1 small sweet potato, peeled, diced, and simmered until soft

Method

1. Combine coconut milk, palm sugar and salt then add all remaining ingredients. Add a few ice cubes and serve.

Serves 4

AVOCADO SHAKE (ES APOKAT)

Ingredients

4 ripe avocados, halved and flesh removed

1/2 cup palm sugar syrup (see page 74)

4 tablespoons condensed milk

1 tablespoon lime juice

3 cups ice cubes

Method

1. Combine avocado flesh with all other ingredients and purée in a blender until smooth. Serve in 4 individual tall hi-ball glasses.

Serves 4

fried banana

BLACK RICE PUDDING (BUBUR INJIN)

Ingredients

1¹/₂ cups black glutinous rice
4–4¹/₂ cups water
1 pandan leaf
¹/₂ cup palm sugar syrup (see below)
coconut milk or ice cream to serve

Palm sugar syrup

1 cup grated palm sugar or brown sugar
¹/₂ cup water

Method

1. Rinse rice under cold running water for 1–2 minutes or until water is clear.

2. Combine rice, water and pandan leaf in a large saucepan. Bring to the boil and simmer over low heat for 40 minutes. Add syrup and cook for a further 10 minutes or until rice is tender and liquid has been absorbed.

3. To make syrup, combine sugar and water in a small saucepan. Bring to the boil and simmer for 8–10 minutes.

4. Serve pudding with coconut milk or ice cream.

Serves 4–6

BANANA AND COCONUT CAKE (KUE PISANG DAN KELAPA)

Ingredients

125g butter, at room temperature
1 cup caster sugar
2 eggs
3 ripe bananas
1/2 cup lemon juice
1 1/2 cups self-raising flour
1/2 teaspoon bicarbonate soda
1/2 teaspoon ground cinnamon
1 cup desiccated coconut

Method

1. Preheat oven to 180°C. Lightly grease a 20cm cake tin and line the bottom with baking paper.

2. Combine butter and sugar in a mixing bowl. Cream butter and sugar together until light and fluffy. Add eggs, one at a time, and beat well after each addition.

3. Place bananas in a food processor with lemon juice. Blend until very mushy. Stir bananas through mixture. Add flour, soda, cinnamon and coconut. Stir until combined.

4. Spoon mixture into prepared cake tin and bake in preheated oven for 40–45 minutes or until a skewer comes out clear. Leave cake to cool for 10–15 minutes then turn out onto a cake rack.

5. Cut into wedges and serve with cream or ice cream and fruit.

Serves 6–8

There are a few pastes and Indonesian instant spice mixes available in Chinese stores. Sambal ulek also called sambal oelek is readily available in supermarkets.

BASIC SPICE PASTE (SAMBAL)

Ingredients

4 French shallots, chopped

4–6 small red chillies, deseeded

2 cloves garlic

2 teaspoons fresh ginger, chopped

1 lemongrass stalk, chopped

Method

1. Prepare spice paste by grinding all ingredients with a mortar with pestle or in a food processor. If using a food processor add a little oil to process.

CHILLI SAMBAL (SAMBAL BAJAK)

Ingredients

4 French shallots, chopped

4 small red chillies, deseeded and chopped

2 cloves garlic, chopped

4 candle nuts

1 teaspoon terasi

1 1/2 tablespoons peanut oil

1 tablespoon tamarind concentrate

1 tablespoon palm sugar or brown sugar

Method

1. Crush or pound shallots, chillies, garlic, candlenuts and terasi with 2 teaspoons peanut oil in a mortar with pestle or a food processor. Process until smooth. Heat remaining oil in a frying pan or wok. Add paste and stir-fry for 1–2 minutes. Add tamarind and sugar. Place paste in an airtight container in the refrigerator and it will last 8–10 days.

TOMATO SAMBAL (SAMBAL TOMATO)

Ingredients

2 French shallots, peeled

4 small red chillies

2 tomatoes

2 tablespoons lime juice

pinch of salt

2 tablespoons chopped basil leaves

Method

1. Finely slice shallots, chillies and tomatoes. Stir in lime juice, salt and chopped basil.

SOY AND CHILLI SAMBAL (SAMBAL KECAP)

Ingredients

2 tablespoons soy sauce

1 tablespoon water

2 tablespoons lemon juice

1 medium-sized red chilli, deseeded and sliced

1 French shallot, sliced

1 clove garlic, crushed

Method

1. Mix all ingredients together.

VINEGAR SAMBAL (SAMBAL CUKA)

Ingredients

1/4 cup roasted peanuts

2 French shallots, chopped

3 medium red chillies, deseeded and chopped

2 cloves garlic

2 teaspoons peanut oil

1/4 cup white vinegar

1 teaspoon palm sugar or brown sugar

Method

1. Crush or pound peanuts, shallots, chillies, garlic and oil in a mortar with pestle or a food processor. Mix together with vinegar and sugar.

FRIED SHALLOTS (BAWANG GORENG)

Ingredients

10 French shallots, peeled

1/3 cup vegetable oil

Method

1. Thinly slice shallots. Dry with a paper towel.

2. Heat oil in a wok. Add shallots and fry until golden. Drain on paper towel and store in an airtight container.

CUCUMBER PICKLES (ACAR SEGAR)

Ingredients

1 tablespoons white vinegar

2 1/2 tablespoons white sugar

1 teaspoon salt

2 1/2 tablespoons hot water

1 medium cucumber, peeled, seeded, cut lengthwise then sliced

Method

1. Mix vinegar, sugar, salt and water until sugar dissolves, then combine with cucumbers and allow to rest for 1 hour before serving.

PICKLED CUCUMBERS AND BEANSPROUTS (DABU-DABU KENARI)

Ingredients

250g medium cucumber, peeled and sliced

1 cup bean sprouts, blanched

4 French shallots, finely sliced

3 red chillies, sliced

4 sprigs basil

50g *kenari* nuts or raw almonds, peeled and coarsely ground

3 tablespoons lime or lemon juice

1/2 teaspoon white sugar

1/2 teaspoon terasi, toasted

1/2 teaspoon salt

Method

1. Arrange cucumber and bean sprouts on a plate and scatter with shallots, chillies and basil. Combine nuts, lime juice, sugar, terasi and salt, adding a little warm water to make a thick sauce. Pour sauce over vegetables and serve.

QUICK PEANUT SAUCE (SAUS KACANG CEPAT)

Ingredients

1/2 cup crunchy peanut butter

1/2 cup water

2 teaspoons sambal ulek

1 teaspoon sweet soy sauce (kecap manis)

2 teaspoons lemon juice

Method

1. Combine peanut butter and water in a small saucepan. Stir over low heat until sauce thickens. Remove from heat and stir in sambal ulek and kecap manis and allow to cool before adding lemon juice.

PICKLED SHALLOTS (ACAR BAWANG)

Ingredients

2 tablespoons white vinegar

1 teaspoon salt

1 1/2 tablespoon white sugar

3 tablespoons warm water

24 French shallots, peeled and sliced

Method

1. Mix all ingredients except shallots, stirring until sugar dissolves. Combine with shallots and sliced chilli (optional). Leave for 2–3 hours before serving.

SPICED COCONUT WITH PEANUTS (SERUNDENG)

Ingredients

2 teaspoons peanut oil

1/2 teaspoon ground cumin

1 teaspoon ground coriander

1/2 teaspoon galangal powder

1 tablespoon tamarind concentrate

1 cup shredded coconut

1/2 cup roasted peanuts

Paste

1 French shallot, chopped

1 clove garlic, chopped

1 teaspoon terasi

Method

1. Crush or pound ingredients for paste in a mortar with pestle or process in a food processor. Heat oil in a wok or frying pan. Stir-fry paste for 1–2 minutes. Add cumin, coriander and galangal, and stir-fry until aromatic. Add tamarind and coconut and stir-fry over low heat until golden. Stir in peanuts.

2. Store in an airtight container for 1 week. Serve cold as a garnish. Keeps about 2 weeks.

PEANUT SAUCE (SAUS KACANG)

Ingredients

1/3 cup peanut oil

100g raw peanuts

1 clove garlic

2 French shallots

1/2 teaspoon terasi

salt

2 teaspoons chilli sauce or sambal ulek

1/2 teaspoon brown sugar

1 1/2–2 cups water

lemon juice to taste

Method

1. Heat 1/4 cup oil in a wok. Add peanuts and fry for 4–5 minutes or until golden. Drain on paper towel. When peanuts are cool, crush in a mortar with pestle or process in a food processor.

2. Crush or pound garlic, shallots, terasi and salt to a paste. Heat remaining oil in a saucepan and cook paste for 1 minute or until aromatic. Add chilli sauce, sugar and water. Bring to the boil, add peanuts and simmer for 20–25 minutes or until sauce is thick. Add lemon juice.

Anchovies, dried (ikan teri): Small salted dried anchovies are used to season some dishes. They are available in most Chinese stores. Unless they are very tiny, anchovies are usually about 2.5cm long. Discard the heads and any black intestinal tract before frying.

Banana leaves: Can be purchased at fruit shops or Chinese supermarkets. They are used for steaming food. The food is usually wrapped in the banana leaf like a parcel. If you cannot buy banana leaves, aluminium foil can be used instead.

Basil (daun selasih, daun kemangi): Two varieties of this fragrant herb are found in Indonesia, generally added to dishes at the last minute for maximum flavour. *Daun kemangi* has a lemony scent, while *daun selasih* is more similar to sweet European basil, which can be used as a substitute.

Beancurd (tahu): Is sold in cakes and is compressed to form a hard cake. It is harder than tofu and darker in colour. Beancurd is available in supermarkets and Chinese supermarkets.

Beans (buncis): The common bean available in Indonesia is the snake bean, also called, runner or long bean. Green beans can also be used. Snake beans are available in both supermarkets and fruit shops.

Candle nut (kemiri): This is a round nut like a macadamia nut. Candlenuts are available in Chinese shops. Substitute with macadamia nuts or almonds.

Carambola, sour (belimbing wuluh): This pale green acidic fruit about 5–8cm long, grows in clusters on a tree. The fruit, a relative of the large, five-edged sweet star-fruit, carambola is used whole or sliced to give a sour taste to some soups, fish dishes and sambals. Sour grapefruit or tamarind juice can be used as a substitute.

Cardamom (kepulaga): About 8–12 intensely fragrant black, seeds are enclosed in a straw coloured, fibrous pod. Try to buy the whole pod rather than cardamom seeds or powder. For maximum flavour, bruise lightly with the back of a cleaver to break the pod before adding to food.

Cassava (ubi kayu): The root of this plant, and the tender green leaves, are both used as a vegetable. The root is also grated and mixed with coconut and sugar to make a number of cakes. Fermented cassava root is added to some dessert dishes, while the dried root is made into small balls (tapioca) and used in the same way as pearl sago. Substitute spinach for cassava leaves.

Celery (seledari): The celery used in Indonesia is different from the Western variety. Indonesian celery has slender stems and particularly pungent leaves and is often referred to as 'Chinese celery' abroad. It is used as a herb rather than a vegetable.

Chillies (cabai, cabe or lombok): Indonesians mostly use small red chillies which are known as bird's eye chillies. These chillies are small and very hot. When deseeding and cutting chillies it is best to wear gloves because the juice can burn your skin.

Chilli paste (sambal ulek or oelek): This is a basic chilli paste, made from crushed chillies.

Chives (kucai): Coarse chives, with flat leaves about 30cm long, are used as a seasoning. Although the flavour of the chive is more delicate, spring onions can be used as a substitute.

Cinnamon (kayu manis): The thick, dark brown bark of a type of cassia is used in Indonesia. It is not true cinnamon. The latter is more subtle in flavour and considerably more expensive. Always use cinnamon quills, not ground cinnamon.

Cloves (cengkih): This small, brown, nail-shaped spice was once found only in the islands of Maluku. Cloves are used in cooking less frequently than one might expect, but add their characteristic fragrance to the clove-scented cigarettes or *kretek* throughout Indonesia.

Coconut milk (santan): Indonesians use fresh coconut in cooking, but it is easier to use tinned or powered coconut milk.

Coriander (ketumbar): Both ground coriander and coriander seeds are used in Indonesian cooking. Coriander seeds are small like peppercorns but lighter in colour.

Cumin (jintan): Together with coriander and pepper, this small beige elongated seed is one of the most commonly used spices in Indonesia. Take care not to confuse it with fennel.

Curry Leaves (daun kari): Available fresh in some fruit shops.

French shallots (bawang merah): A relative of the onion family which has small bulbs covered in brown, yellow or pink skin.

GLOSSARY

Galangal (laos, lengkuas): This is a member of the ginger family. Dried galangal and galangal powder is also available in Chinese supermarkets.

Garlic (bawang putih): Indonesian garlic cloves are usually smaller and less pungent than the garlic found in many Western countries. Adjust the amount to suit your taste.

Kecap Manis: This is a thick sweet soy sauce. Available in supermarkets and Chinese supermarkets.

Kenari nuts : The canari nut is quite oily and comes from Maluku – substitute with almond.

Lemongrass (serai, sereh): Available in supermarkets and fruit shops. To prepare, slice the white bottom part and crush into a paste. Bruise the top half and tie it in a loose knot. Add the top half to a curry for flavour.

Lime (jeruk nipis): Several types of lime are used in Indonesia. The most fragrant is the leprous or *kaffir* lime (*jeruk purut*). It has virtually no juice but the double leaf is often used whole or very finely shredded, while the grated skin is occasionally used in cooking. Round yellow-skinned limes, slightly larger than a golf ball, and small, dark green limes are used for their juice. If limes are not available, use lemons.

Palm sugar (gula merah, gula Jawa): Comes in a hard round block. It is available in supermarkets. Substitute with brown sugar.

Pandan leaf (daun pandan): This is a fragrant leaf and is used to flavour desserts and curries. It is usually tied in a knot. Available in some fruit shops.

Peanuts (kacang tanah): These are ground up (either raw or cooked) and used to make sauces. Deep-fried peanuts are a very common garnish or condiment. Do not salt fried peanuts before cooling then storing or they will become soggy.

Prawns, dried (ebi): Used to season some dishes, these should be soaked in warm water for 5 minutes before use and any shell discarded. Choose dried prawns that are bright pink in colour and avoid any that look grey or mouldy.

Salam leaf (daun salam): A subtly flavoured leaf of a member of the cassia family. The flavour bears no resemblance whatsoever to that of bay leaves, which are sometimes suggested as a substitute.

Salted soya beans (tauco): Salty and with a distinctive tang, this Chinese ingredient is used to season some dishes and to make a savoury side-dish or sambal.

Sambal ulek: Indonesian salty chilli paste available in stores.

Soy sauce (kecap manis or kecap asin): Two types of soy sauce are used in Indonesia: thick sweet soy sauce, which is most frequently used as a condiment, usually with added sliced chillies, and the thinner, saltier light soy sauce.

Spring onion (daun bawang): Sometimes known as scallions or, in Australia, as shallots, this popular herb is often used as a garnish and to add flavour to many dishes.

Star anise (bunga lawang, pekak): An 8-pointed star-shaped spice, dark brown in colour, with each point containing a shiny brown, round seed. It has a strong aniseed or licorice flavour.

Tamarind (asam jawa): Is used to give a sour taste to a dish. It is available in a block, and needs to be mixed with water. It is easier to use concentrate which comes in a screw-top jar. Available in Chinese supermarkets.

Tapioca (telur ubi kayu) see Cassava.

Tempeh (tempe): This is a compressed cake of soya beans. Available in supermarkets and Chinese supermarkets.

Terasi (trasi, blachan, belachan, shrimp paste): This comes in a hard block. When cooking cut off required amount and add to paste or, to pre-cook terasi, dry-fry a small amount wrapped in foil. Available in Chinese supermarkets.

Turmeric (kunyit): This is a member of the ginger family. Fresh turmeric is available in some fruit shops and Chinese supermarkets. Ground turmeric is readily available.

Yam bean (bangkuang): Used in salads and some cooked vegetable dishes; water chestnuts make an acceptable substitute.

CONVERSION TABLE (All spoon measurements are level)

Approximate quantities rounded to usable units. Metric cup measures are available in most countries; it is advisable to use them instead of guessing or using a kitchen cup. The conversion quantities given are approximate, rounded to the most practical unit; they are not as accurate as the metric measurements. My recipes use the Australian tablespoon that is 20g. Be aware that American tablespoons measure 15g, so an additional level teaspoon of the ingredient must be used to achieve the same result.

Liquids
1 metric cup = 250mL
½ metric cup = 125mL
⅓ metric cup = 80mL
¼ metric cup = 65mL

Spoons
1 teaspoon = 5g
1 tablespoon = 20g

Dry ingredients
50g = approximately 2oz
100g = approximately 4oz
250g = approximately 8½oz
450g = approximately 16oz

Oven temperature
140°C/275°F/gas mark 1
160°C/325°F/gas mark 3
180°C/350°F/gas mark 4
200°C/400°F/gas mark 6
240°C/475°F/gas mark 9